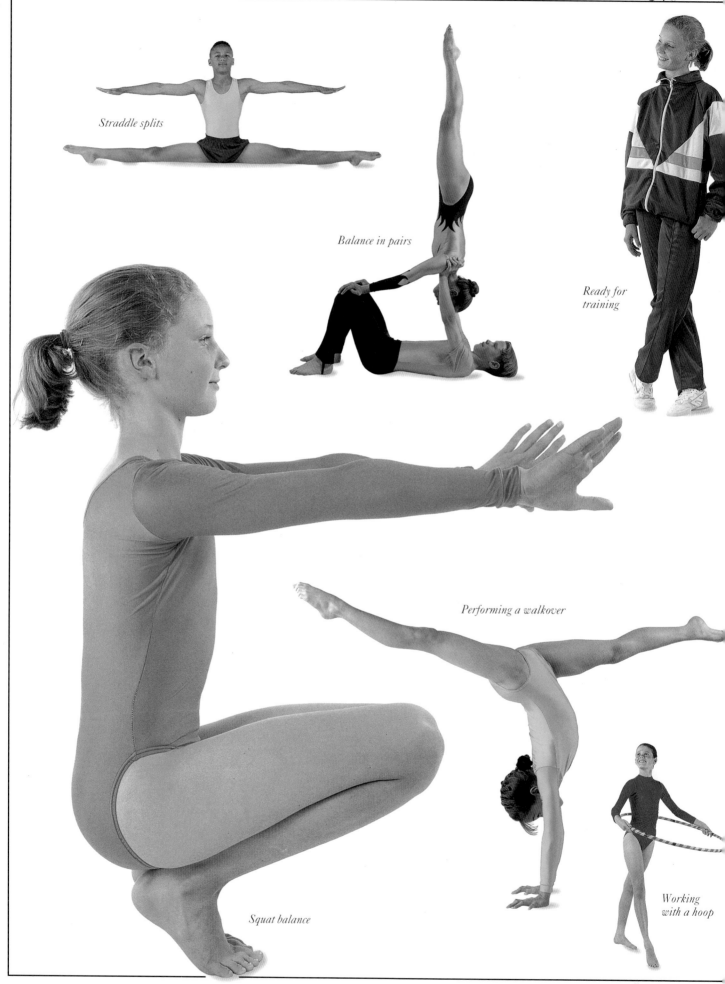

Straddle splits

Balance in pairs

Ready for training

Squat balance

Performing a walkover

Working with a hoop

Finishing position

Cartwheeling

 # SUPERGUIDES

GYMNASTICS

JOAN JACKMAN

FOREWORD BY
SHANNON MILLER

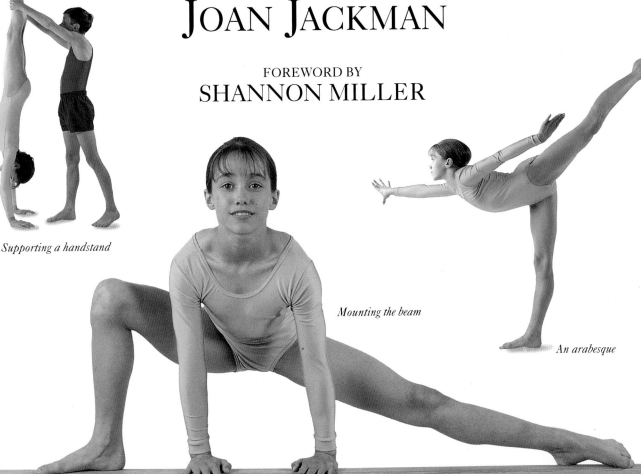

Supporting a handstand

Mounting the beam

An arabesque

V-sit

DK

DK PUBLISHING, INC.

DK www.dk.com

*Moving into a
shoulder balance*

LONDON, NEW YORK, MUNICH, MELBOURNE and DELHI

Project editor Stella Love **Art editor** Lesley Betts

Photography Ray Moller

Picture research Anna Lord

Production Catherine Semark

Deputy editorial director Sophie Mitchell

Deputy art director Miranda Kennedy

The young gymnasts
Nick Addo, Ben Brown, Lucy Carnan, Adam Edwards,
Becky McCormack, Chloe Prangnell, Cheryl Wilcox

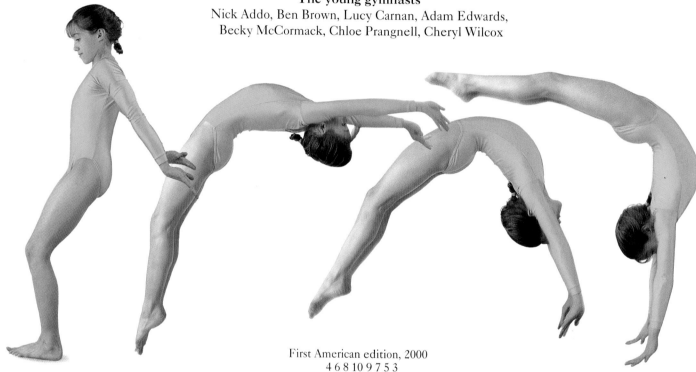

First American edition, 2000
4 6 8 10 9 7 5 3

Published in the United States by
Dorling Kindersley Publishing, Inc.
375 Hudson Street
New York, New York 10014

Copyright © 1995, 2000
Dorling Kindersley Limited

First published as *The Young Gymnast*, 1995

ISBN: 0-7894-5430-0

Color reproduction by Colourscan, Singapore
Printed and bound in Italy by L.E.G.O.

See our complete product line at
www.dk.com

Contents

To all young gymnasts

"**G**YMNASTICS is much more than a beautiful sport to watch. It also develops your muscles, your sense of balance, and your flexibility. With the improvement in your physical health comes a wonderful sense of self-esteem. Whether you just take classes or decide to compete, your mind and your body will benefit from the exercise and discipline required. Competition brings even greater rewards. You learn poise and the ability to control your fears. You get to travel and meet lots of other kids, and you learn to take instruction well. You'll probably find that your schoolwork improves – even though you have less time for homework – because you become much better organized. But most important, training and competing are fun! I know you'll really enjoy reading this book and I hope it will help you discover and appreciate the exciting world of gymnastics.**"**

Shannon Miller

At the World Championships
Shannon Miller with the gold medal she won when she took the all-around title at the 1993 World Championships. At the same event, she also won the individual apparatus titles for the asymmetric bars and floor exercises.

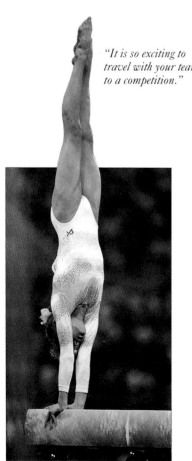

"It is so exciting to travel with your team to a competition."

"If one or more of your scores counts toward a team trophy, you feel terrific!"

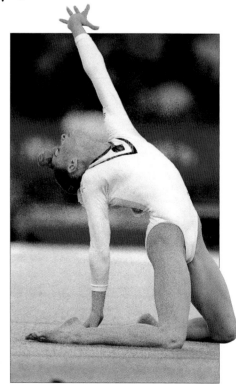

"Each day is a new adventure in learning, both mentally and physically."

History of gymnastics

Swinging [ri]ngs was an [O]lympic event [fo]r women.

FROM PAINTINGS, pottery, and other historical evidence, we know that forms of gymnastics were practiced more than 3,000 years ago in ancient Egypt and later in Greek and Roman times. As the Roman Empire declined, so too did gymnastics. For many centuries, only wandering entertainers kept acrobatic and juggling skills alive. Then, early in the 19th century, two men – F. Jahn of Germany and P. Ling of Sweden – introduced new ways to exercise, from which modern gymnastics developed.

Acrobatic entertainers
At the end of the 17th century, acrobats often performed during the intermission of a play.

A gymnasium in 1859
[H]ere you can see some early forms of the apparatuses [u]sed today, such as the vaulting horse, which was shaped [li]ke a real horse until 1930. Many of the exercises in [p]rogress are to develop arm and shoulder strength.

Clubs and dumb-bells

Rings

Wall bars are still seen in many gyms today.

Parallel bars

A girls' school gymnasium in 1900
Clubs and dumbbells were used to develop strength and flexibility in the arms and shoulders. There were few exercises for the rest of the body.

Gymnastics today

[T]oday, gymnastics and its various disciplines are a [p]opular sport for girls and boys of all ages. You may [ch]oose to work in general gymnastics only, learning [so]me skills from all the disciplines and training [ju]st for fun. Or, you may decide to specialize [i]n just one discipline.

Holding a balance

[G]irls' artistic gymnastics
[T]his is a competitive discipline in [w]hich you work on your own on [ea]ch of four pieces of equipment – [th]e asymmetric bars, floor, [be]am, and vault.

Making a bridge

Boys' artistic gymnastics
This is a competitive discipline like girls' artistic gymnastics, but boys work on six pieces of equipment – the floor, pommel horse, rings, parallel bars, horizontal bar, and vault.

Balancing with a partner

[R]hythmic gymnastics
[T]his is another discipline for girls. It [re]quires great flexibility and involves [m]any dance movements that are [m]ade while working with small [ha]nd apparatuses – ball, hoop, [ro]pe, ribbon, or clubs.

Working with a hand apparatus

Sports acrobatics
Boys and girls take part in sports acrobatics. Balances form a major part of this sport, but it also involves gymnastic skills, such as acrobatics, dance movements, and tumbling.

Starting gymnastics

GYMNASTICS IS a very exciting sport. If you have enjoyed gymnastics in school and want to improve, or if you have been thrilled by gymnastics on television, you may feel inspired to join a club and start training. Start by finding out what clubs are available in your area and what sort of classes they offer. You will not need any special clothes when you begin. Wearing a T-shirt and shorts will be suitable at first, but eventually you will need to get the sort of clothing shown here. Your coach will advise you when you are ready to buy special equipment such as hand guards.

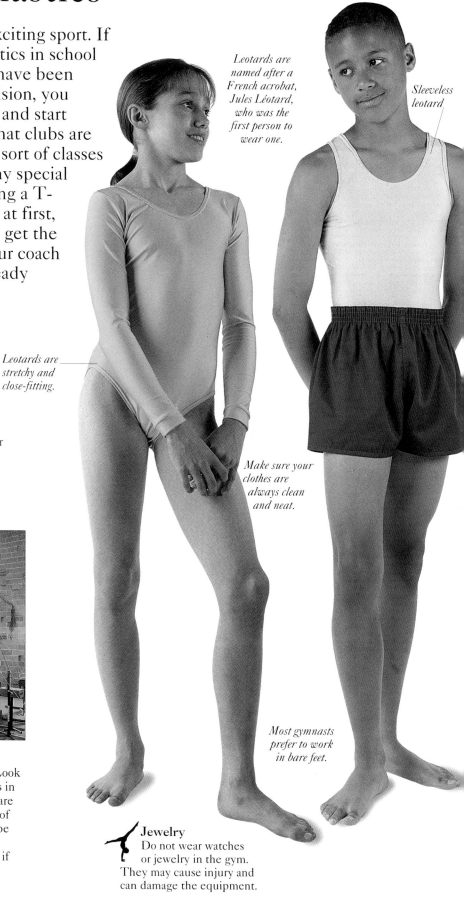

Leotards are named after a French acrobat, Jules Léotard, who was the first person to wear one.

Sleeveless leotard

Leotards are stretchy and close-fitting.

Make sure your clothes are always clean and neat.

Most gymnasts prefer to work in bare feet.

Girls' clothes

Girls wear leotards. Leotards are made of stretchy fabrics and fit closely. This helps your coach see the body shapes you make and how you move during practice so that your mistakes can be corrected. Leotards are ideal for gymnastics because they are comfortable to wear and allow you to move freely.

Joining a club

Go and watch a club session before you join. Look to see if the gym is clean and the equipment is in good condition. Try to find out if the coaches are well qualified and ask if the club is a member of the sport's governing body. Check if you will be able to take awards once you are a member, or enter competitions if this interests you. Then, if you are satisfied, join the club and get started.

Jewelry
Do not wear watches or jewelry in the gym. They may cause injury and can damage the equipment.

Boys' clothes

Boys wear shorts over a sleeveless leotard for practice sessions. In competition they may wear shorts for floorwork and vaulting, but on the other pieces of equipment, boys must wear long tights.

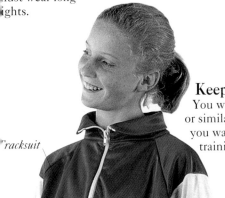

Keeping warm

You will need a tracksuit or similar clothes to wear as you warm up and during training if it is very cold.

Tracksuit

Your club may have tracksuits and leotards in the club's own colors.

Boys' and girls' training

In the early stages of training, boys and girls learn many of the same basic skills and use much of the same equipment. Some of the boys' apparatuses require great strength and the boys only begin to specialize when they are older and stronger. Girls have to be strong and flexible, too, but they can produce simple sequences on their apparatuses at a young age.

Ready for training

Pack your bag carefully so that you always arrive at the gym with everything you need.

Hair

Your hair should be neat and tidy, and not falling in your eyes. If you have long hair, tie it back or braid it so that it is off your face and cannot swing to hit either you or your coach.

Boys' hand guard

A small metal ridge helps the boys grip the bars.

Girls' hand guards

Hand guards

Gymnasts usually wear hand guards for work on the bars and rings. Hand guards prevent blisters from forming and help the swinging and circling movements required.

Chalk

Chalk

Many gymnasts put chalk on their hands and feet. The chalk stops their hands from getting sticky with perspiration and prevents their feet from slipping on the mats.

Warming up

Every session will start with a warm-up. This is a series of exercises to make your heart beat faster, increase your breathing rate, loosen your muscles and joints, and make you more flexible, preventing stiffness and injury. The warm-up will make you ready to work.

Wrists and fingers do a lot of work. Warm them up well.

There are exercises for every part of you.

Bend, stretch, shake, and circle your feet and ankles.

Warm-up exercises

The exercises used in the warm-up should include every part of your body. You will be able to practice some of them at home, which will help make you flexible and strong.

Apparatuses

APPARATUSES FOR artistic gymnastics have changed greatly over the years. In the early days there were no set measurements for the equipment. Then, almost 50 years ago, rules were agreed on about the apparatuses to be used in Olympic and World championships. Since then, the apparatuses have been constantly improved and updated. The new materials used, and advances in training, have helped make the spectacular gymnastics you see today possible. You may see some of this equipment in your gym, but before you will be able to start using it, you will have to master some basic skills and improve your strength, stamina, and flexibility.

Scoreboar

Asymmetric bars

Vault runup

Rings
Rings are used only in men's gymnastics, but until 40 years ago women used them, too. Modern rings are 18 cm* (7⅛ in) in diameter and hang 275 cm (8 ft 2 in) above the floor. Here, Travis Romagnoli of Canada shows the strength and control needed for work on the rings.

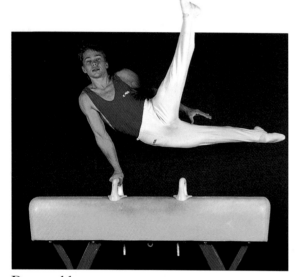

Pommel horse
The pommel horse is 160 cm (5 ft 4 in) long and stands 115 cm (3 ft 10 in) high. It is used only for the pommel exercise in men's gymnastics. Here you can see Vitaly Marinich of Ukraine in action. He travels along the horse, supported on his hands, as he makes smooth, swinging movements with his legs and body.

Parallel bars
The parallel bars are part of the men's equipment. The gymnast has to travel above and between the wooden bars, on his hands, upper arms, or on one arm, as in this Diamidov turn shown by Andrei Kan of Belarus.

*Metric measurements are considered standard for gymnastics equipment.

Vaulting horse
The vaulting horse is used by men and women. It is 160 cm (5 ft 4 in) long, 35 cm (14 in) wide, and its height is adjustable. The top is slightly padded and covered in suede or another nonslip material.

Women use the horse at a height of 120 cm (4 ft), and men at 135 cm (4 ft 5 in).

Balance beam
A beam exercise lasts between 70 and 90 seconds. It is performed only by women. The beam is 5 m (16 ft 3 in) long but only 10 cm (4 i wide. Its height is adjustable, but for competition it is set at 120 cm (3 ft 11 in). The surface of the beam is padded to make it slightly springy. This helps cushion the gymnasts as they land on it.

Floor

Floor exercises take place on a carpeted square 12 m (40 ft) wide, built on a springy base. The edge of the area is marked by a white line and surrounded by a wide, sloping, safety border.

Beam

Parallel bars

Floor

Vaulting horse

Competition arena

This arena is set out for a major artistic gymnastics competition. Each piece of equipment is surrounded by safety mats. Tables for the judges are placed where the judges will have a clear view. The judges enter the scores for each exercise into an electronic score box and the scores are relayed to a central computer.

Rings

Chalk bucket

Score box

Safety mat

Asymmetric bars

Fan Di of China shows a popular mount on the asymmetric bars. These bars are used only in women's work. An exercise should include swings, circles, and handstand positions. An advanced gymnast will include release and catch moves – letting go of the bar, performing a move in the air, then catching the bar again.

Horizontal bar

Valeri Lioukin of Ukraine performs on the horizontal bar. The bar is 240 cm (7 ft 10 in) wide and used only by men. It is set at 275 cm (8 ft 2 in) from the floor and to start an exercise, a gymnast's coach will lift him up. Much of the work is similar to the women's work on the asymmetric bars and includes spectacular circles around the bar, and release and catch moves.

Springboard

A springboard is a device that helps you rebound upward. It is used for vaulting and for mounting other apparatuses, such as the beam and asymmetric bars. It is 120 cm (4 ft) long and rises about 20 cm (8 in) from the floor.

You can adjust the height of most apparatuses.

Making shapes

THE SHAPES you can make with your body are the essence of gymnastics. Whether on the floor, on the bars, on the beam, or in midair, each gymnastic movement is made up of specific shapes. It is the skill of moving through one shape to the next that makes gymnastics so exciting to watch. It is important that you understand the form of all the shapes and learn to use your whole body to create each one – as your body becomes stronger and more flexible, you will still be building on these basic shapes.

Kneeling on one leg
This shape can be used as a balance on the floor or the beam. Make sure your raised leg is well stretched, and lift your head.

You can vary this shape by changing the position of your raised leg, or lifting one arm.

Dish
The dish is a strengthening move that will improve your posture. Lift your legs and arms, tightening your stomach muscles.

Lie on your back and raise your arms, shoulders, and legs from the floor.

Press your lower back flat on the floor.

Arch
The arch is similar to the dish, but in reverse. Lie on your front and pull in your buttock muscles as you lift your head, arms, upper body, and legs off the ground. Keep your head between your arms and make sure your legs are straight.

Extend through your arms and legs.

Straddle splits
It will take lots of time to become flexible enough to make this shape. Keep your back straight as you stretch your legs wide apart. Aim to press your legs farther back each time you try this.

Hold your arms out horizontally, or stretch them up above your head.

The bridge will require practice to perform really well as you will need to develop a flexible back and shoulders.

Your head should stay between your arms. Try not to let your chin strain upward.

Do not let your knees roll forward.

Improving flexibility

To condition your body and become a good gymnast will take years of practice. Your flexibility will improve with training, and you will gradually be able to extend the range of shapes you can make and hold comfortably. Here, Hui Lan of China demonstrates the flexibility of her back and shoulders.

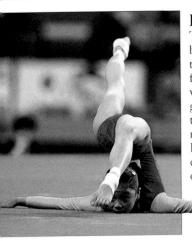

Rear support

This position requires strength to hold. Your arms must be straight and directly under your shoulders. Pull in your stomach and buttock muscles so that your body makes a straight line from your head to your feet.

Be sure to match the angle of your hands.

Front support

Like the back support, this shape demands that you hold your body in a straight line. Make sure that you keep your arms straight and that your hands are only shoulder-width apart.

Check that your hands are each in the same position.

Be patient

Do not force your body into any positions that hurt or feel strained. Be patient – with practice your body will become more flexible and you will be able to achieve most of the shapes shown here soon.

Straighten your legs so that they slope from your hips to the floor in a straight line.

From this position, you will eventually be able to kick your legs over, one at a time, to come back onto your feet in a move called a bridge kickover.

Keep your feet and legs together.

Shapes in the air

Make sure you understand exactly what shape you are trying to show as you go through each stage of a movement. Here Annika Reeder of Great Britain shows a dramatic shape as she leaps high in the air.

Bridge

To make a bridge, start by lying on your back with your knees bent up and your feet flat on the floor, close to your buttocks. Bend your elbows and place your hands on the floor on either side of your head. Your fingers should point toward your feet and your elbows should point to the ceiling. Push up strongly from your hands and feet to raise your body into position, and straighten your legs.

Keep your feet flat on the floor.

Rolls and rolling

ROLLING IS is an important basic gymnastic skill that can be used in many different ways. In a roll, the weight of the body transfers from one body part to another, which makes rolling movements useful for linking a variety of shapes and skills together. On the floor, a roll itself can make an effective low shape. And because rolls can be fast or slow, they can be used to change the pace of an exercise. If you watch gymnastics, you will see rolls being used creatively in all the gymnastic disciplines.

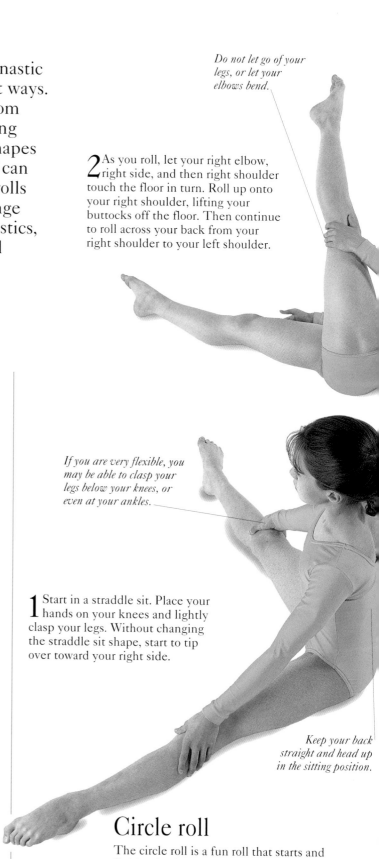

Do not let go of your legs, or let your elbows bend.

2 As you roll, let your right elbow, right side, and then right shoulder touch the floor in turn. Roll up onto your right shoulder, lifting your buttocks off the floor. Then continue to roll across your back from your right shoulder to your left shoulder.

If you are very flexible, you may be able to clasp your legs below your knees, or even at your ankles.

1 Start in a straddle sit. Place your hands on your knees and lightly clasp your legs. Without changing the straddle sit shape, start to tip over toward your right side.

Keep your back straight and head up in the sitting position.

Log roll

The log roll is a useful move to turn smoothly from your front to your back, or from your back to your front. As you roll, your body weight must change from one body part to another in a controlled way, and each shape must be shown clearly.

Hold your arms shoulder-width apart.

Lift your legs and press them together.

1 Start in an arch shape and begin to roll onto your side. Be careful to maintain the tension in your body and keep your arms and legs fully extended.

2 On your side, your body should be in a straight line with your buttock and stomach muscles pulled in, and your head between your arms. Continue rolling over.

3 As you roll onto your back, move into a dish shape with your arms and legs lifted off the floor. Press your lower back flat to the floor.

Circle roll

The circle roll is a fun roll that starts and finishes in the same position, but facing in a different direction. Interesting shapes and patterns can be made if you work with a partner or a group of four people.

Forward rolls

The shape of a forward roll is used in many gymnastic moves, so it is important to learn to roll correctly from the beginning. It is much harder to correct bad technique once it has become a habit.

Use your arms to help you balance.

Roll on the back of your head and neck.

Push off with your hands to bring yourself onto your feet.

1 Balance on the balls of your feet in a neat squat position.

2 Put your hands on the floor, tuck your head in, and start to roll.

3 A strong push from your feet will roll your body over.

4 Reach out with your arms to help you come back into a squat position.

As you roll onto your shoulders, the weight of your legs in the air will help you keep moving.

Make sure your toes are pointed at all stages of the roll.

3 Continue rolling down your left side and elbow onto the left side of your buttocks. Let the weight of your legs carry you over as you start sitting up from your left side.

4 Finally, roll across your buttocks, bringing your right leg down to the floor. You should finish the roll in the straddle position in which you started, but facing the opposite direction.

Starting and finishing positions

Forward rolls can start and finish in a great variety of positions.

The roll may be taken from standing instead of squatting.

Practice coming back onto your feet and standing up at the end of the roll without using your hands to help you up.

A forward roll from a balance, such as an arabesque, is a useful linking move in a floor or beam exercise.

Roll onto the back of your head.

Pull up through your supporting leg.

Relax your shoulders.

Do not let your hips twist.

A strong finishing position can make the roll an effective movement in a simple sequence.

Backward rolls

FROM THE SIMPLE shape of a backward roll, many other moves develop. The tightly tucked position of both backward and forward rolls is the basis of the tucked somersault. You will need to work on the move into, and out of, the tucked rolling position on the floor before you will be able to go on to achieve the jumps and vaults that include the somersault action. Backward rolls are a basic skill to master, but like other movements that travel backward, you will probably find them harder to learn initially than movements that go forward.

Rolling on a slope

Using a sloping surface can help you learn a new skill. In the backward roll, it helps you turn over onto your feet. Working up a slope may also be used in training sessions to improve your strength and stamina.

Keep your knees and feet together and use your stomach muscles to pull up your legs.

Point your toes, extending the stretch through your feet and ankles.

Tuck your ch. onto you ches

A foam wedge or a springboard covered with a ma. make good sloping surfaces to practice on.

How to do a backward roll

A backward roll needs to have enough speed and force to carry the movement through to the finish. Toppling backward into a tight tuck position will make you start to roll, rounding your back will help keep the motion going, and a strong push with your hands will carry the roll over to bring you back onto your feet.

Start with your head up and eyes looking straight ahead.

Use your arms to help you balance.

Your feet should be together and toes pointed.

2 Curl your back so that you roll along it from your buttocks to your shoulders. Bend your elbows and point them up to the ceiling as you put your hands on the floor on either side of your head.

Keep your elbows high and close to your knees. Do not let them collapse onto the floor.

1 Start in a well-balanced squat position with your knees together and your back straight. To begin the movement, let your heels drop toward the floor so that you are off balance and you start to roll back onto your buttocks.

Keep your knees together.

Let your heels drop to start the rolling movement.

Start and finish positions

Like the forward roll, the backward roll can start and end in many different positions, which is why it is such a useful linking movement. To finish kneeling on one knee, let one leg extend behind you as you come out of the roll. The straddle stand can be used to start or end the roll. You may find it fun to experiment with other start and finish positions.

Hold your head up.

Stretch your back leg out behind you.

Keep your back straight and parallel to the floor in this straddle stand position.

The slope helps you lift your hips high and feel your weight moving onto your hands.

Learn to push up strongly through your hands and arms as your feet come down to the floor.

Keep your chin tucked in to keep your weight off the top of your head.

The finishing position can then be made on the floor.

Hand position

The push from your hands is the key stage of the roll. Make sure you position your hands correctly.

Tucking up

Tuck your chin down onto your chest as you start to roll over in both backward and forward rolls.

Relax your shoulders. Try not to let them hunch up as you hold the finishing balance.

Put your palms flat on the floor, and point your fingers toward your shoulders.

3 Push strongly from the floor and begin to straighten your arms. This will lift your hips high so that your body can roll over your head as your feet come down to the floor.

Your knees should not touch the floor.

4 The push off the floor as you straighten your arms should be strong enough to carry you through the final turning stage of the roll and back onto your feet.

Finish on your toes.

19

Balances

A BALANCE is a shape that a gymnast makes and holds, poised on just part of the body. Good form is essential for balance work. To maintain a moment of stillness, a gymnast must have complete muscle control. A good balance will show flexibility, poise, and a clear body line. So, whether you are holding a basic shape or a difficult balance, be aware of your whole body – from the expression on your face through to the position of your fingertips and toes.

Beam balance
Shannon Miller shows a steady balance on one leg with the other leg raised in preparation for her next move. Each shape helps to make an effective beam exercise.

On one foot

Use your arms to help you balance.

Do not let your hips twist.

1 One of the simplest balances on a small body part is on one foot. Stand with good posture and raise one leg in front of you, bending your knee.

2 Carry your raised leg around to the side, keeping the knee bent. Pull up through your supporting leg.

3 Stretch and lift your free leg out to the side to hold a strong, balanced position.

Rising onto the ball of your foot or lifting your free leg higher will make this balance much more difficult.

V-sit balance

1 This seat balance starts easily, but becomes more difficult as you lift your legs and arms. Start by sitting with your hands and toes resting on the floor.

Look up at your toes.

2 Stretch your legs high in front of you and use your hands to steady yourself.

Do not let your back sag.

3 Finally, us your stoma muscles to hel you lift your arms up to complete the V-shape.

Only a small part of your buttocks remains on the floor.

Shoulder stand balance

Your body should stay flat on the floor until the final lift into the balance.

Press down wi your fingers to steady yourself.

1 To start, lie on your back with the small of your back and the palms of your hands pressed into the floor.

2 Bend your legs up over your chest. Push down with your hands and start to lift your hips off the floor.

3 Stretch your legs up vertical and extend out through you toes to hold the balance firmly.

Arabesques

An arabesque is an elegant balance on one leg with the other leg raised behind and the arms stretched out in harmony. In its many forms, it is widely used in girls' gymnastics. Arabesques can be performed with the front leg straight or bent, and the back leg can be kept low or held high, but in all cases, your head and body should be positioned to form an attractive line.

First arabesques
When you first start to practice arabesques, you will not be able to raise your leg very high. It is more important to concentrate on forming the right body shape.

Stepping into an arabesque
With practice you will be able to go into an arabesque from another movement.

Try to link the stages into a continuous movement from the start through the step, and into the arabesque position.

Bend your front knee.

Make sure your supporting foot does not roll inward.

1 Stand in a clear start position with your arms up, your legs straight, and your feet together. Pull up through your body.

2 Take a lunge step, bending the knee of your front leg. Carry your arms down in a smooth and controlled movement.

Arabesque with supported leg
You will need to be flexible and strong to hold an advanced arabesque position like this one.

1 From a firm stance on one leg, clasp the knee of your raised leg with one hand. Keeping your knee bent, rotate your leg out to the side and then back behind you.

Hold your leg around the knee.

Let your eyes follow the line of your arm.

Turn the palm of your hand down.

2 Keep holding your raised leg as you lean forward, stretching it up behind you. As you do so, carry your opposite arm forward.

Only take the leg as high as you comfortably can without twisting your hips or losing your balance.

This arm follows the line made by the raised leg.

Keep your back arched, your shoulders relaxed, and your head lifted.

Arm positions
Arm positions for an arabesque can be varied. Both arms can be held high, out to your sides, or with one arm carried forward and one arm back. Whichever position you choose to take, the line of the arms should make the arabesque look balletic and graceful.

3 Let your weight move forward over your supporting leg as you straighten it and carry your back leg up behind you.

21

Headstands and handstands

BALANCING ON your head and hands is an important basic skill used in both boys' and girls' gymnastics. If you watch gymnastics, you will soon spot headstands and handstands being used in all sorts of ways, and with a great variety of leg positions. Because they are so widely used, you will probably start learning these skills early in your training. At first you will need help from your coach to reach and hold these balances. Then you will start to develop your skill by changing your leg positions and linking the balances with other moves.

Tucked headstand

A tucked headstand starts from a crouch. Position your head and hands on a mat and move your feet in to bring your hips over your head. With bent knees, lift up your feet. When you can balance like this, try straightening your legs into a stretched headstand.

Lift your hips high.

Keep your elbows bent.

Balance on the front edge of your head at about your hairline.

On the bars
The handstand shape is required for swings and circles around the bars, shown here by Tatiana Gutsu of Ukraine.

Keep your head between your arms.

Hold a straight body line.

Stretch your arms up, keeping your shoulders down.

Stretch your back leg as you kick up.

Supported handstand
You will see the handstand shape used in floor, bar, beam, ring, and vault work. Before you can start to use it with other skills, you must learn to hold it as a perfect upright balance. Practice with support from your coach or another gymnast until you can perform a handstand and hold it unaided as a balance.

Push off from your back foot to lunge forward.

Bend your front knee into a lunge position.

A partner can help by supporting you firmly at hip-level as you kick up into the handstand.

1 At first you will start a handstand from a standing position. With your arms stretched above your head, take a long lunge step forward and look to the point on the floor where you are going to place your hands.

2 As your hands go to the floor, kick up your back leg and push up from your front leg, straightening the knee. The upward swing of your back leg, combined with the pushing action from the front leg, will carry your front leg off the floor.

Push up strongly through your front leg and foot.

Head and hand position
Make a triangle with your head and hands on the mat. Place your hands shoulder-width apart and spread your fingers.

Equal weight
Spread your weight equally on your head and hands.

Straight leg headstand
Going into the stretched headstand with straight legs is a more advanced move. Start by kneeling, and position your head and hands on the mat.

Straighten your legs to push your hips up. Start to drag your feet toward your hands.

Keep your legs straight and lift them up until they are parallel to the floor.

Carry your legs up into the fully stretched headstand position.

Grip the floor with your fingers to hold yourself steady.

When you reach the handstand position, your partner can change holds, and support you at the ankles.

3 As your second leg swings upward, press both legs together and stretch your feet and ankles. You should try to hold your body so that your ankles, knees, hips, shoulders, and hands are all in a straight line.

Your partner can help correct your body position.

Giving support
Move in to support your partner as the legs swing up. Do not back away.

Look at your hands.

Place your hands on the floor shoulder-width apart.

Pull in your stomach and buttock muscles.

Do not let your back hollow or sag.

Spread your fingers and grip the floor to help steady your balance.

Cartwheels and round-offs

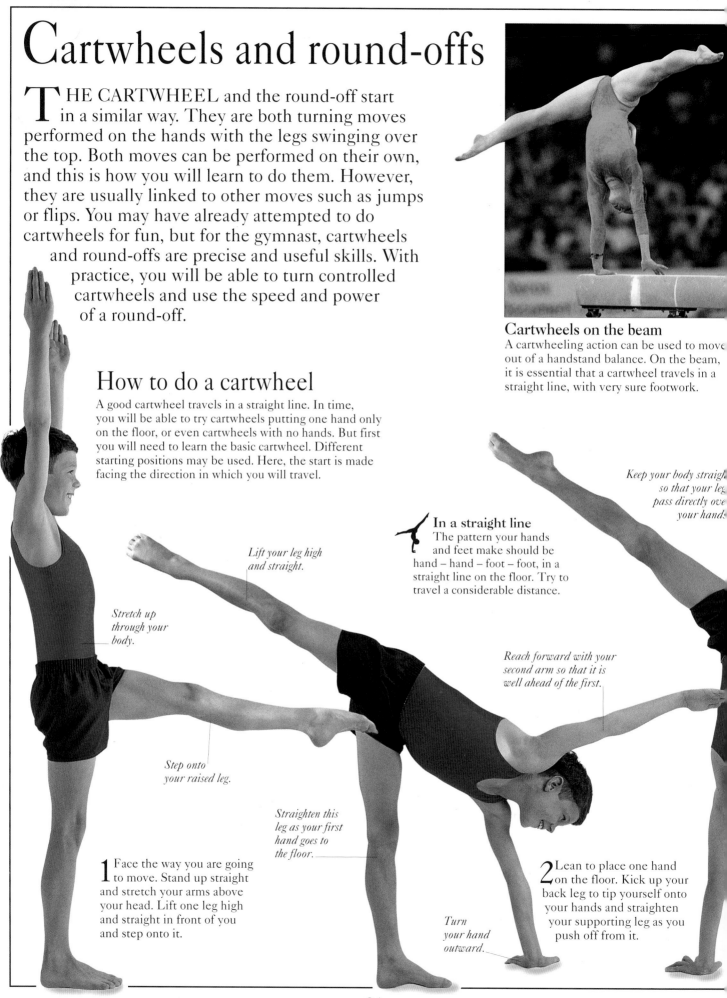

THE CARTWHEEL and the round-off start in a similar way. They are both turning moves performed on the hands with the legs swinging over the top. Both moves can be performed on their own, and this is how you will learn to do them. However, they are usually linked to other moves such as jumps or flips. You may have already attempted to do cartwheels for fun, but for the gymnast, cartwheels and round-offs are precise and useful skills. With practice, you will be able to turn controlled cartwheels and use the speed and power of a round-off.

Cartwheels on the beam
A cartwheeling action can be used to move out of a handstand balance. On the beam, it is essential that a cartwheel travels in a straight line, with very sure footwork.

How to do a cartwheel

A good cartwheel travels in a straight line. In time, you will be able to try cartwheels putting one hand only on the floor, or even cartwheels with no hands. But first you will need to learn the basic cartwheel. Different starting positions may be used. Here, the start is made facing the direction in which you will travel.

Lift your leg high and straight.

In a straight line
The pattern your hands and feet make should be hand – hand – foot – foot, in a straight line on the floor. Try to travel a considerable distance.

Keep your body straigh[t] so that your leg[s] pass directly ove[r] your hands

Stretch up through your body.

Reach forward with your second arm so that it is well ahead of the first.

Step onto your raised leg.

Straighten this leg as your first hand goes to the floor.

1 Face the way you are going to move. Stand up straight and stretch your arms above your head. Lift one leg high and straight in front of you and step onto it.

Turn your hand outward.

2 Lean to place one hand on the floor. Kick up your back leg to tip yourself onto your hands and straighten your supporting leg as you push off from it.

Stretch up and face forward.

Hands down
Put your second hand down out of line with your first hand.

The round-off
The round-off is a move that is used to build up speed in a sequence, leading into a jump or another agility. It starts like a cartwheel, but includes a quarter turn, and your legs come together so that you land on two feet, facing the opposite way.

Swing your legs up as if to cartwheel.

Your hands are already starting the turn.

Bring your legs together in the air.

Push off with your hands.

Swing your arms up to control your landing.

Land on two feet.

Face the way you are moving. Step forward and spring onto our hands, one after the other.

2 As your first hand goes to the floor, kick up your back leg. Swing your other leg up and bring them together.

3 A strong push from your hands will help you snap your legs down so that you land on two feet.

Keep your legs in a wide split.

Hold your arms level and your shoulders down.

plit your legs wide part in the side andstand osition.

Keep your knees straight and stretch your feet and ankles.

3 Place your other hand on the floor in line with the first. As your legs swing upward, you should turn sideways into a handstand position.

Your hands should be shoulder-width apart on the floor.

Stretch your leading leg to the floor.

End your cartwheel standing sideways to the way you started, with your feet apart.

4 From the handstand position, continue turning. Push off from your first hand and bring your leading leg down to the floor, in line with your hand.

5 A strong push-off with your hand, together with the movement of your legs coming down, one after the other, should bring you back to a standing position.

Push off the floor to return to your feet.

Finish in a stretched standing position.

Flic flacs and walkovers

AS YOU MAKE progress with your training, you will start to learn some more advanced moves. All the work you have done so far will help you now. At first the idea of falling back and landing on your hands may seem frightening. Backward movements such as the walkover and flic flac are difficult to learn, but they are essential moves if you are to continue improving your gymnastic skills. With help from your coach through all the preparatory stages, you will find them exciting skills to master.

Back walkover

The back walkover is usually used in conjunction with other moves, and ca be performed quickly or slowly.

Reach for the floor.

Extend your leading leg.

Push off from this foot.

1 Start with your leading leg raised and move your arms backward, letting your head drop between them and arching your back.

2 Lift your leading leg h and when your hands reach the floor, push up through your supporting l

How to do a flic flac

Never try this without your coach. All gymnasts aim to do a flic flac, but it is an advanced move and there are many preparatory skills to learn first. The flic flac is often used to build up speed for another move, such as a somersault, as well.

First flic flacs
At first, you will be taught to flic flac from a standing position to finish standing on two feet. Then you may learn to do it from a back walkover or a round-off.

Swing your arms up over your head.

Straighten your legs.

Preparatory skills
Do not attempt the flic flac until you have mastered all the preparatory skills and your coach is there to help you.

Bend your knees.

Push off the floor through your legs and feet.

Point your toes and extend through your ankles.

Start to look for your landing spot on the floor.

1 Start in a standing position with your feet together, and bend your knees. Lean back in an off-balance position, taking your arms back behind you.

2 Spring off the floor with a strong push from your feet and legs, and swing your arms upward over your head. Straighten your legs and let your hips lift up.

3 Let your legs drive your body upward and backward, but make sure you keep your head back between your arms as you start to reach for the floor.

how a wide splits shape in the handstand position and maintain it as your leading leg reaches for the floor.

Keep your legs fully stretched.

A back walkover is often followed by a flic flac.

The back walkover may be used as an advanced way to move into splits. Bring your leading leg down between your hands and slide it forward to finish sitting in the splits position.

3 Your legs should be very straight and reach a splits position as you come over into a handstand.

4 Keep the second leg high and straight as the first leg comes down to the floor. Then carry the second leg down to finish the move.

Walkover on the beam

You will often see walkovers used in both beam and floor exercises. Lisa Grayson of Great Britain shows perfect control as she performs a back walkover on the beam.

Keep your feet together and do not let your knees bend.

Don't bend your knees until your feet touch the floor.

Stand with good posture and your arms stretched up.

Your legs start to swing over your head.

spread your ngers slightly s you land on ur hands.

Land on two feet and bend your knees.

Push off with your hands.

4 Keep your body arched as your hands touch down, with your legs and lower body still following through on the line f your flight.

5 From the arched position, swing your legs and feet over, and snap them down sharply toward the floor. Keep your upper body straight.

6 As your feet touch the floor, let your knees and ankles flex to cushion your landing. Stand up straight to finish.

Jumps and leaps

JUMPING AND leaping movements are used by all gymnasts. A jump usually takes off from two feet and lands on two feet. In a leap, the takeoff is from one foot, with the landing on the other foot. Together, you can use jumps and leaps to link acrobatic skills or as part of your dance movements in your floor and beam sequences. Good vaulting and mounts onto the beam or bars also demand strong jumping actions. Experiment, and you will find that you can make lots of different shapes in the air by varying your leg and arm positions as you jump and leap.

Stag leap

The stag leap is a popular and attractive move that you will often see in floor and beam work. It takes its name from the shape the back leg makes as it bends and lifts. You can vary the leap by straightening your front leg in the air, or by taking both your arms upward.

Point your toes.

Lift your back leg as high as you can.

Keep your back straight.

Swing your arms upward.

Try to get good height from the push-off.

Swing you front le hig

1 You can practice this move as a standing jump from two feet. Later, you can use one or two steps to turn it into a leap traveling forward. Start with good posture and take one step. The leg that you step onto will be the leg that you kick up behind you.

2 As you step, swing your other leg forward into a high leap. Push off from your stepping foot and swing your arms up to gain as much height as possible as you travel forward and upward.

Step forward, ready to leap.

Push off from this foot.

Shapes to make

You can make hundreds of different shapes
in the air when you jump. The higher
you jump, the more time you will have
to make the shape. Always flex your
knees as you land, and try to land softly.

*Turn your head
slightly over your
front shoulder.*

*Raise your arms
to shoulder-height.*

*Hold your
head up
and relax
your
shoulders.*

*Do not let your
hips twist.*

*Your front leg lifts,
then descends to a
soft landing.*

*Make sure your
back stays
straight.*

Straddle pike jump

In the air, straddle your
legs and stretch them out.
At the same time, bend
forward from your hips to
make the pike position.

*Extend through
your feet and
ankles.*

3 Lift your back leg high
and bend it up behind
you to make the stag shape.
Bend your front knee and
take one arm forward and
the other one back.

*Land softly on
your front foot.*

Tuck jump

Bend your knees up tightly
in front of your body as you
jump. Use the swing of your
arms upward to help you
travel up, and not along.

*Keep your
head lifted.*

*Bring your
knees up to
your chest.*

*Stretch your
feet and
ankles.*

Split leap

Gina Gogean of Romania
shows a split leap on the
beam. A strong upswing
with her arms has helped
her achieve great height in
the leap, and by keeping
her arms up, she makes a
strong shape that adds to
the feeling of height.

Star jump

Try to make a
symmetrical shape
in a star jump. Your
arms should stretch
out at the same angle
as each other, and so
should your legs.

*Stretch out through
your arms, body,
and legs.*

*Show a wide
straddle position
with your legs.*

Making a sequence

ONCE YOU have learned a few skills, you can start linking them together to make a sequence. In a major competition, artistic gymnasts perform two exercises on each piece of equipment. First, they all have to perform the same sequence as each other in the compulsory, or set, exercise. Then, in the voluntary exercise, they can include some of their favorite skills. When you make up a sequence, include the things you can do well, and then try to put in some changes of speed and height to make your work really interesting to watch.

Kick your leading leg up as you go into the round-off.

Stretch up through your body.

Start this sequence ready to move into a round-off.

Begin the turning movement on your hand

Shapes and joins
Try to show clear shapes at every stage of your sequence, and join each move smoothly.

A girl's floor exercise

Girls perform floor exercises to music, and an exercise lasts between 70 and 90 seconds. Par of the skill of a good performance is to interpr the mood of the music with the dance steps, jumps, leaps, balances, and turns you use. Th sequence shown here includes a series of agilities, and includes two changes of directio

A boy's floor exercise

A boy's floor exercise should be designed to show strength and control. You will see that many of the same skills are used in both boys' and girls' sequences, but boys do not perform to music. So, although the boys' exercises must be artistic, they use jumps and strength elements rather than dance elements.

Hold the inside of your heel.

Make your dive as high and long as you can.

Keep your legs together and straight.

Take your arms back, ready to swing forward.

In competition, a held balance must be included in the boys' floor exercise.

1 This sequence starts with a Y-balance. Hold your balance for two seconds.

2 Bring your free leg down and turn as you step forward onto it. Spring from both feet into a dive.

3 Swing your arms forward to give you lift and let your legs drive you upward and forward into a dive forward roll.

Look ahead t your landin poin

Reach for the floor.

Dive roll
You must only attempt the dive roll on a gymnastics floor with good mats to land on.

Swing your second leg up and snap both legs down together to land.

Bring your legs together.

From the acceleration of the round-off, spring into a flic flac.

Look for the floor.

Start to split your legs, ready to land on one foot.

Bring one leg over first.

As your hands reach the floor, swing your legs over, showing a split position clearly.

Point your toes.

Finish with a smile even if you made a mistake.

With your chin on your chest, tuck into a forward roll.

From your handstand, tip into a forward roll.

Kick into a handstand balance.

Land your flic flac on one foot, bringing your second leg down behind.

From the roll, come straight to a standing finish position with poise and good posture.

Push with your hands.

Keep your arms straight.

Land on this foot.

6 Then kick up to a steady handstand.

Point your toes.

7 Move your hands in quarter-turns to turn your body.

8 Finish your handstand pirouette facing the opposite way.

4 Land on your hands, tuck your head in, and roll on the back of your neck.

5 Roll onto your feet and come up to stand.

Press your legs together.

Tuck down into the roll.

Stretch your arms up to help you come up to a standing position.

Keep your body straight.

Do not let your back hollow.

Take your weight on your hands.

Roll on the back of your neck and shoulders.

Spread your fingers and grip the floor.

Walk around on your hands.

Vaulting

VAULTING IS one of the most exciting events in gymnastics, and top gymnasts now perform vaults of amazing difficulty. They often include somersaults and turns, and even takeoffs with a turn so that the vault is performed backward. When you start to vault, you will have to practice all the preparatory stages, beginning with exercises using the springboard and jumping onto and off the vaulting horse, learning to land safely.

Down to earth
For safety, always land on two feet when you jump from a height or vault.

Swing your arms up straight.

3 Make sure that you hold a straight handstand shape all the way over.

Keep your feet together and your legs and body extended.

Handspring vault

A handspring is a simple vault. In this sequence, you can see the stages of the vault: the takeoff, the flight onto the horse, the repulsion stage – or the handspring itself, the flight off the horse, and the landing. When you start to practice vaulting, you will discover that every vault can be divided into these stages.

1 Start with a strong, fast, even run up to the springboard. From the run, take a hurdle step so that your feet land together on the springiest part of the board.

2 Swing your arms forward and upward as you make the jump from the springboard. Keep your body extended in the flight onto the horse.

Your head shoul stay neutral, neither tilted up or down.

Take off with an upward jump from two feet.

At takeoff, your feet should be slightly in front of your body.

Hands on
Your hands should be shoulder-width apart as they make contact with the horse. Spread your fingers slightly to take your weight.

Vaulting hors

The springiest part of the board is about 20 cm (8 in) from the raised end.

The horse can be lowered for junior gymnasts.

Women's vault

Women always vault widthways across the horse, which is known as side-horse vaulting. Here, Svetlana Boguinskaya of Belarus performs a Yurchenko full twist – many gymnastic moves are named after the gymnast who first performed them internationally. From this height she will complete the twist and straighten out to land.

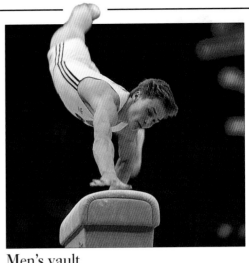

Men's vault

Men always vault along the length of the horse, which is known as long-horse vaulting. In competition, the men get only one attempt at their chosen vault. Valeri Lioukin of Ukraine shows a Kasamatsu vault.

ur hands come off the rse as soon as possible.

With good body tension, you may show a dish shape.

Keep your arms stretched above your head.

5 From your extension off the vault, land on the balls of your feet, quickly lowering your heels to the floor and flexing your knees, ankles, and hips.

Extend your body.

4 As you come over the horse, push off, extending through your whole body to start your flight off the horse.

Try to get a good distance between the horse and your landing point.

You will lose points for an unsteady landing.

Hands off

Try to push off to get height in your flight off the horse and show space between your hands and the top of the horse.

Vaulting in competition

In a major competition, the value of each type of vault depends on how difficult it is to perform. A difficult vault with turns or somersaults will be marked out of 10.00 points. A handspring is considered to be a simple vault and is marked out of a lower scale. Even if you perform it perfectly, you cannot score a full 10.00 points.

Flex your knees and ankles.

Land with your feet together.

The balance beam

THE BEAM, or balance beam, is used only in girls' gymnastics. In competition, gymnasts have to perform a sequence of balances, jumps, agilities, and turns. Each move should flow freely into the next, with the gymnasts only pausing to hold the balance positions. Some of the skills may be simple to perform at floor level, but they become much more difficult when executed on the beam, and many gymnasts fear it. You will need to spend long hours perfecting your technique on the floor to build up enough confidence to move freely on this apparatus.

The mount can be made to the side or end of the beam.

Mounts and dismounts
There are many ways to get on and off the beam to start and finish an exercise. A springboard may be used to mount the beam and, in competition, bonus points may be awarded for a difficult mount such as a front somersault. But points will be lost for a fall, so it is better to be safe than sorry.

On the beam
When you have practiced and mastered skills on the floor, the next step will be to work on a low beam or bench until you are controlled and very confident. Then you will be able to move on to a practice beam surrounded by safety mats, which can be built up to the height of the beam, and gradually removed as you make progress.

Lift your leg high and complete the Y shape with your free arm.

Keep your arms level with each other.

Hold the balance still for two seconds.

Do not let your body twist.

Before trying any advanced balances and jumps, you will learn to walk, turn, and sit on the beam.

Extend your foot.

Hold your head up and keep your shoulders down.

Grip the sides of the beam with your fingers.

V-sit
A beam exercise must show moves low to the beam, such as this V-sit. From this position the gymnast could push up into a bridge shape or lie back into a backward roll.

Y-balance
A Y-balance is a difficult shape to hold, but attractive balances are an important part of a beam exercise. Keeping your head up and fixing your eyes on a point in the distance will help you hold a balance.

The difficulty of a balance can be increased by performing it up on your toes.

Beam practice

...colored foam strip ... sometimes used to ...ark the width and ...ngth of the beam ...o that gymnasts can ...ractice moves for the ...eam or work out a ...equence safely at ...oor level.

Jump with confidence and try to land lightly.

A cabriole jump

Neat footwork is very important on the beam. Most work should be performed on your toes.

In competition

Shannon Miller holds a handstand balance on the beam. In competition, points are awarded for the difficulty of the moves shown, but it is wise not to include moves you cannot do well. Points are deducted for lack of technique, and you will lose 0.5 of a point for a fall.

W-jump

It is important to show a variety of jumps and leaps during the exercise. The elegant W-jump is a favorite with gymnasts on the beam.

Keep your head up and your eyes fixed on a point in the distance.

Jump sequences

Competitions require a sequence of two or more jumps. Practice linking different jumps, one after the other, with no step in between.

Try to show as much height as possible when you jump.

2 The shape that you make in the air defines the sort of jump you are making. In the W-jump, one leg stretches forward horizontally, with the heel of the other foot tucked up beneath you.

3 Let your knees flex to help you land softly but steadily. Use your arms to help you maintain your balance.

Steady landings

In a competition, the judges will look for steady landings. Points will be deducted if you wobble or lose your balance.

1 Try to show good posture, with your head up and back straight at all stages of the jump. Start in a poised position, and with one step, take off from both feet.

Flex your knees as you land, ready to jump again, or go into your next move.

Rhythmic gymnastics

RHYTHMIC GYMNASTICS is a branch of gymnastics for girls. If you like the balletic side of gymnastics and enjoy working to music, you will like learning rhythmic skills. Rhythmic work takes place on a carpeted floor area, 12 meters square (40 ft). The gymnasts perform dance movements to music while using hand apparatuses. At first, you will spend a lot of time learning to use the apparatuses. In time, you will be able to throw, catch, and use them to make interesting shapes, and be able to link them with leaps, balances, turns, and a variety of low and high moves.

The swivel helps keep the ribbon from tangling.

Silk ribbon

Keep your eyes on the ribbon.

Raise your arm above your head.

Keep the ribbon moving all the time.

Working with the ribbon
Ribbon work is very attractive to watch as the ribbon circles and spirals around the gymnast. Use a large arm movement to keep the ribbon moving along its entire length. The ribbon should not touch any part of your body, nor become entangled in any way.

Stretch up into an elegant arabesque balance.

The ribbon is 7 m (23 ft) long and attached to a wand.

Swivel

Apparatuses
There are five pieces of equipment and, in time, you will learn how to handle each of them. Many gymnasts find the clubs difficult to use and you will probably learn to use them last.

Balls should be 18-20 cm (7-8 in) in diameter, and weigh 400g (14 oz).

Wand

Hoop

Hoops are usually made of plastic. They should be between 80 cm and 90 cm (31-35 in) in diameter.

Wooden or plastic clubs

Rope

The rope may be knotted at the ends but must have no handles. Its length depends on the height of the gymnast.

Group work
As a rhythmic gymnast, you may perform on your own or work in a group of six. In group work you can use different pieces of equipment – here the Bulgarian team is using hoops and balls. The team is shown in its finishing position at the end of the group sequence.

Hoop sequence

You can use hoops in many ways to create an effective sequence. You can swing them around your body, roll them on the floor, throw them in the air, or jump through them.

Swing the hoop around your waist.

Turn your head slightly.

Balance on one leg.

Look at your free hand.

Catch the hoop with both hands, then let one side drop.

Stay up on your toes.

Jump through the hoop.

Carry your free arm up as you jump.

Carry the hoop out to the side to finish.

Rope work

Ropes can be used for skipping steps. They can also be thrown, folded, or wrapped around you. The simple moves shown here will give you some ideas to practice.

Hold your arms well out from your body.

...p on one ...t as you ...n the rope ...kward.

Point your toes as you skip.

Watch the rope.

As the rope swings up, stop it by lifting up your hands.

The loop of rope will fall back.

Stretch out your hands and catch the rope in the middle.

Stay up on your toes. This foot position is called demi-pointe.

Now you have folded the rope into four, ready to use in different ways.

Balance on one leg and twirl the ends of the rope.

Ball balance

This move with the ball is called a spiral. Here it is taken from kneeling and rises to finish in an arabesque. The ball must stay balanced on the palm of your hand. It must not touch your wrist, or be grasped in your fingers.

Kneel on one leg, rest one hand on the floor, and start with the ball held low in front of you.

Straighten your arm.

Carry the ball out to the side.

Bend your body in a full side bend.

Keep your arm straight and circle the ball behind you.

Bring the ball around to your other side.

Hold a graceful arm position.

Lift the ball high.

Look up at the ball.

Pull up through your body.

Rise into an arabesque balance.

Rise on demi-pointe.

Sports acrobatics

SPORTS acrobatics developed from acrobatic circus performers and balancing acts seen in shows. Today, the sport has two branches: pair group work and platform tumbling. For pair group work, you will need to master gymnastic skills such as jumps, leaps, turns, and acrobatic moves. You will also learn to achieve spectacular balance positions. Pair group routines are performed to music on a springy floor 12 meters (40 feet) square. They include both balance elements and individual skills.

Keep your body upright and very still.

You can use a variety of arm positions. Hold your arms out sideways, upward, or take one arm forward.

Into position
Move slowly and steadily into each balance position. When you are perfectly steady, hold the balance for at least two seconds.

Support your partner under one knee and the thigh of her extended leg.

Stretch your back leg.

Straighten your legs.

Hold your body in a straight line.

Keep your arms straight to support yourself.

Spread your feet slightly apart.

Base and top
In pair work, the gymnast on the floor is called the base. The supported partner is called the top. In this simple balance, the base supports the weight of the top on his knees and arms.

Entries and exits
You can make your work interesting and attractive to watch by using imaginative ways to get into, and out of, the balance positions.

Take your partner's weight equally on both your legs.

Press your back and arms into the floor to steady the balance.

Groups of four
Boys and men may compete in groups of four. In this Bulgarian group, the mid-position is balanced only on his arms, while the top holds a one-armed balance.

Stag balance
The stag balance shows the essence of mixed pair work. The elegance and grace of the top contrasts with the strength and steadiness of the base. To reach this position, the base bends his legs. Once the top is in place, the base straightens his legs to lift the balance.

Balances must be held for two seconds.

Boys may perform as a pair or as a group of four.

Counterbalance

A counterbalance is when you use your weight against your partner's weight. Both of you must keep good body tension as you lean away from each other. When you first try this balance, ask for help setting the top into position.

Look at your partner.

Stretch out your free arm in line with your body.

Don't let your head drop back.

Clasp hands firmly.

Maintain body tension.

Lean back.

A Ukrainian boys' pair shows a difficult one-armed balance.

Point your toes.

You can vary this balance by using different leg positions.

Bend your knees.

A firm hold

It is essential that you both take a firm hold. Grip hands and clasp your fingers.

Spread your feet apart.

Three exercises

In competition, the teams perform three exercises. The first is called balance and includes a set number of balances. The next exercise is called tempo, in which the base throws and catches the top. The third exercise includes both balance and tempo moves.

Hand position

Cup your partner's shoulders in the heels of your hands.

Keep your back straight.

Straight arms

Shoulder balance

The shoulder balance is simple and stable. The base has a large part of his body on the floor and the top has several points of support. From here, the top may move her hands to her partner's hands or arms and extend to an advanced balance only on the arms.

Lift up your head.

Stretch and lift your legs.

Press your back flat to the floor.

Your arms, and those of your partner, should be straight and shoulder-width apart.

Palm to palm

Support with palm to palm contact and use your fingers to add control.

Stand with your feet apart to give you a wide base.

Straddle lever balance

This is an advanced balance that requires great strength from the base. The top rises into a lever position with her legs widely straddled and lifted.

Girls' trio

Girls can compete as a pair or in a group of three. Here, a Latvian trio shows a complicated counterbalance, forming an exciting shape.

Tumbling

PLATFORM TUMBLING is an equally important branch of sports acrobatics and, like pair group work, boys and girls both take part. The gymnasts, or tumblers, work on a springy strip of floor 25 meters (82 feet) long and 1.5 meters (5 feet) wide. The tumblers travel in a straight line and accelerate as they perform a series of fast agilities, joining them one after the other without pausing. To become a tumbler, you will have to start by mastering basic gymnastic skills. Then, as you make progress, you will work on round-offs, flic flacs, and somersaults and learn to link them with other agilities.

Starting a tumble run
A springboard may be used at the start of a run. It will help you add height and speed to your opening move.

Tumble runs

Here you can see two different tumble runs. In competition, each tumbler performs three separate runs: one with straight moves, one twisting, and one combining straight and twisting moves.

Step onto your raised leg.

1 This run starts with a handspring.

Swing your back leg up.

Move onto both hands.

Bring your legs together.

2 Push off strongly with your hands to lift yourself from the floor.

Land on one foot.

3 Step straight into a round-off on your free leg.

Stretch out your free leg.

Scoring in competition

The scores from the tumbler's three runs are added together to make a possible total of 30 points. All the runs must go in one direction from start to finish. If the tumbler falls, or adds an extra step, the run is judged to be finished and no further part of it will be marked.

Safety mats
When you learn acrobatic skills, use plenty of safety mats to cushion any bad landings.

Stretch your lower legs and feet.

2 From the takeoff, tuck into a somersault. Keep your elbows close to your body.

Jump upward using your arms to help the movement.

1 Here, the tumble run opens with a forward somersault from a fast run.

If you land on one foot, you must step into the next move with your free leg. Do not put in any extra steps or pauses.

Open out to land on one foot.

Kick your back leg up.

Stretch out your free leg and lunge onto it.

Reach for the floor.

3 Move straight into a round-off with a lunge step forward.

Keep your head between your arms.

The round-off will turn you around, ready to make the next move backward.

Keep your legs very straight.

Piked back somersault

Every tumble run should finish with a somersault. There are lots of different somersault shapes. They can be made straight, tightly tucked, twisting, or in a piked position, as shown here. They can also be made forward or backward, and even double or triple.

Tuck your knees in to your chest.

Tucked front somersault

The tucked front somersault is a good opening move for a tumble run, and it can land on one or two feet. Like all somersaults, it must be made high in the air to allow time for your body to stretch out to land.

Try to get as high off the ground as possible.

Bend at your waist into the piked position.

Swing your arms up.

Your last move should be a spectacular somersault.

Advanced agilities
Never try an advanced agility such as a somersault or flic flac without your coach there to support and help you.

Your speed should be increasing all the way through the run.

6 From your flic flac, jump upward and backward into a piked back somersault.

7 Land on two feet and stand perfectly still to finish.

Swing your arms up.

Flex your knees.

5 Immediately spring into a powerful flic flac.

Reach for the floor.

4 Snap your legs down together to land on two feet.

Extend through your legs, ankles, and feet.

If you land on two feet, you must take off from two feet into the next move.

Center line

There is a straight line marked along the center of a tumbling track. You will lose points if you do not manage to keep your tumbling movements straight and you start to move away from this line.

Make your somersault as high as you can.

Show a clear body shape in the air.

4 Land on two feet from the round-off and swing your arms up and back.

Keep your legs together.

Swing your arms up to help you take off.

Keep your arms, legs, and back straight.

6 Use the speed of your flic flac to take off into a straight back somersault.

Point your toes.

5 Spring straight into a flic flac, using your legs to drive yourself backward.

Whip your legs down to land on two feet.

Use your legs and feet to drive yourself upward.

7 Finish your tumble standing straight and still. You will lose points for any arm or body movements used to regain your balance.

Competitions

GYMNASTICS lends itself to competition because it is a beautiful and dynamic sport to watch. Competitions can be arranged to suit different age groups and all levels of ability. If you would like to compete, there are many opportunities for you to do so in all branches of gymnastics. At the lowest level, you can simply work to pass on to more advanced levels within your club. Then, you may find it fun to take part in matches arranged between your school or club and other clubs. In this way, you will gradually progress and compete against more experienced gymnasts. At the highest level, there are national and international competitions. Very few gymnasts reach this level, but knowing a little bit about the major events will make them more exciting to watch.

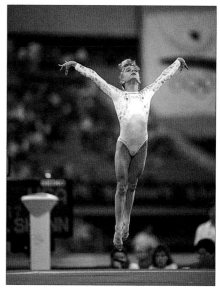

Dance, drama, and dynamics
Shannon Miller uses her talent for dance, dramatic touches, and dynamic agilities to excel in the floor exercise.

Rules and regulations

For every country, the *Fédération Internationale de Gymnastique* (FIG) is the overall governing body of artistic and rhythmic gymnastics. The FIG produces a Code of Points – the rule book for all the high-level artistic and rhythmic events, such as the Olympic Games and World Championships. Sports acrobatics is not yet an Olympic sport. It has its own governing body, the International Federation of Sports Acrobatics (IFSA), which sets the rules for that sport.

Competition program

Throughout the year, each country holds its own competitions. From these, the best gymnasts are selected to be in the national senior or junior teams. Each country also has a program of international competitions that take place both at home and abroad. Even at the international level, some events are arranged for different age groups. There are competitions for a senior team, an under-15 team, and even an under-12 team.

Major international competitions

Olympic Games
These are held once every 4 years and include artistic and rhythmic gymnastics.

Artistic World Championship
This is held every year, but the events included, e.g. team or individual events, are varied in alternate years.

Rhythmic World Championship
This event is held every year.

Sports Acrobatics World Championship
This event is held every year.

Junior World Championships
Separate championships for each of the gymnastic disciplines are held every 2 years.

World Student Games
This competition is held every 2 years and includes artistic and rhythmic gymnastics.

World School Games
This event is held every two years and includes artistic and rhythmic gymnastics.

Judges and judging

In a major artistic competition there are six judges and a technical advisor to watch each exercise. Moves in the exercise are given a value depending on how difficult they are to perform.

Judges use symbols like these as a quick way to note the moves they see in an exercise.

Double turn   *Handspring*   *Arabesque*

The technical advisor adds up the value of all the moves, the content, and the possible bonus points and tells the judges the maximum score that they can give if the exercise has been performed perfectly. From this score, the judges deduct points for any mistakes they have spotted during the exercise.

Handstand   *Cartwheel*   *Back walkover*   *Pik jum*

Rhythmic

In a major rhythmic competition, there are two panels of six judges. Six judges mark the technical content of the exercise while the other six judge the performance.

At the 1993 World Championships in Birmingham, Great Britain

Medal winners
Shannon Miller on the podium with silver medalist Gina Gogean of Romania, and bronze medalist Tatiana Lisenko of Ukraine.

Sports acrobatics

In tumbling and balance work, competitors perform three exercises to score a possible total of 30 points. There are six judges, but the highest and lowest scores are left out. The score awarded for each exercise is the average of the other four scores.

Glossary

During your gymnastics classes, or when watching gymnastics, you may find it helpful to understand some of the following words and phrases.

A

Agility A gymnastic move of an acrobatic nature, such as a cartwheel, as opposed to dance movements or jumps.

Apparatus A piece of equipment on which gymnasts work, or rhythmic gymnasts use.

Artistic gymnastics A competitive sport for girls and boys in which they perform exercises on gymnastics apparatuses.

Asymmetrical When two parts of a whole are not the same. The two bars of the asymmetric bars are at different heights, for example.

B

Balance exercise A sports acrobatics exercise that involves held balances.

Base The name for the gymnast who supports the weight of the other or others in sports acrobatics.

Body tension Contraction of the muscles with no visable change in body shape.

Bonus points Extra points awarded by judges for some very difficult moves.

C

Chalk Magnesium carbonate. Some gymnasts dust it on their hands and feet to prevent slipping.

Code of Points The rule book issued by the FIG for coaches, judges, and gymnasts, from which competition rules are written.

Compulsory exercises Also known as set exercises. Exercises set by the governing body that must be performed exactly as written down and illustrated.

D

Demi-pointe A term used in rhythmic gymnastics to mean "on your toes."

Discipline Rhythmic and artistic gymnastics are gymnastic sports, or disciplines.

Dismount The move you use to get off an apparatus.

E

Element A gymnastic move, or one essential part of an exercise.

Execution The performance of an exercise or move.

Extend To stretch to the maximum.

F

FIG The *Fédération Internationale de Gymnastique* is the governing body of world artistic and rhythmic gymnastics.

Flex To bend in a controlled manner.

Flexibility The ability to bend freely, without strain.

Flight Movement through the air either onto, or from, an apparatus.

H

Hand guards Leather guards to protect your hands when you work on the bars.

Held balance A poised position that you hold still for a moment.

Hurdle step A step from one foot landing on two feet in order to take off from both feet when using a springboard.

I

IFSA The International Federation of Sports Acrobatics is the governing body for that sport.

L

Line The shape made by positioning your body and limbs.

Lunge A position with one foot well in front of the other, with the front knee bent and most of your weight over it.

M

Mount The way you get onto an apparatus. It may be a difficult and daring move to score bonus points.

P

Pike A position in which your body and legs form a V-shape as you raise your legs high and straight, together or straddled.

Pirouette A spin or turn that may be made on your hands or feet.

Posture The carriage of your body, or the way in which you hold yourself.

R

Rebound To bounce from something, such as a springboard.

Release and catch A term used to describe letting go of the bar, performing a move in midair, and catching the bar again.

Rhythmic gymnastics A form of gymnastics for girls only, using small pieces of handheld apparatuses and combining dance and gymnastic moves.

Routine A full exercise consisting of all the moves performed by a gymnast.

S

Score box An electronic device into which judges enter scores to relay them to a central computer.

Sequence A series of gymnastic moves linked together by dance and jumps.

Somersault A full rotation of the body, performed in the air.

Sports acrobatics A gymnastic sport for boys and girls that includes balance work in pairs, trios, and fours, and tumbling work.

Stamina Your endurance, or ability to perform exercises many times without tiring.

Straddle A position with your legs stretched wide apart.

Suppleness The ability to bend all parts of the body well, with flexible muscles.

Symmetrical When the two sides, or parts, of a whole look identical. A star jump forms a symmetrical shape.

T

Technical advisor Also known as the technical expert or scientific technical collaborator. An official who advises the judges of the maximum possible score for an exercise, according to the Code of Points.

Technique The method or way in which you perform a gymnastic skill.

Tempo exercise The sports acrobatics exercise in which one gymnast is thrown or boosted into the air by another.

Top The name for the gymnast in sports acrobatics who is supported by the base.

Tuck A position in which you bring your knees up to your chest.

Tumbling A series of gymnastic agilities joined into a continuous run, without pauses or extra steps between the moves.

V

Voluntary exercises The exercises that a gymnast chooses to perform in competition.

W

Warm-up The essential preparation at the start of every training session to prevent injury. Warm-up exercises make your heart beat faster, increase your breathing rate, and loosen joints and muscles.

Index

Useful addresses

Below are the addresses of the governing organizations in the US and Canada for gymnastics and sports acrobatics. Each publishes a directory of clubs and should be able to help you find one in your area.

US Gymnastics Federation
Pan Am Plaza
Suite 300
201 South Capital Avenue
Indianapolis, Indiana 46225

Tel : (317) 237 5050

US Sports Acrobatics Federation
4700 Pierce Street
Riverside, California 92515

Attention: Roger McFarland

Tel : (909) 785 2084

Canadian Gymnastics Federation
1600 James Naismith Drive
Suite 510
James Naismith Drive
Gloucester
Ontario
Canada K1B 5N4

Tel : (613) 748 5637

Cheryl

Lucy

Ben

Adam

Becky

Chloe

Nick

Acknowledgments

Dorling Kindersley would like to thank the following people
for their help in the production of this book:

All the Young Gymnasts for their enthusiasm and patience during the photographic sessions; Clem Malcolmson of Woking Gymnastic Club, Surrey, for providing the artistic gymnasts and the venue; and all the staff at Woking, especially Sue James, for the advice and practical assistance so willingly given; Jan and Tony Wills of the King Edmund Gym Club, Yate, Bristol for helping with the section on sports acrobatics and providing the sports acrobats; Catherine Smith of Spelthorne School of Gymnastics, Ashford, Middlesex for her guidance on rhythmic gymnastics and providing the rhythmic gymnast; Patsy Burrell of Burrell Designs, for making the leotards; Bernadette Crowley, Linda Martin, and Susan Peach for additional editorial assistance; and Steve Whitlock of the US Gymnastics Federation.

Picture credits
key: B bottom; L left; R right; C center; T top.
Allsport/Gerard Vandystadt: 33TC
Mary Evans: 9CR, 9CL
Gymnova: 10BL
Mansell: 9TL, 9TR
Felipe Sanchez Monsivais: 8BR
Sporting Pictures: 8BL, 20TR, 35TR
Supersport/Eileen Langsley: 8BC, 8TL, 12CL, 12TR, 12CR, 13CLB, 13CRB & 13T, 15TL, 15CR, 22CL, 27TR, 29BL, 33TR, 36BR
Endpapers: Agence D.P.P.I./ Philippe Millereau
Back jacket: Supersport/ Eileen Langsley BR